A NOTE TO PARENTS

When your children are ready to "step into reading," giving them the right books is as crucial as giving them the right food to eat. **Step into Reading Books** present exciting stories and information reinforced with lively, colorful illustrations that make learning to read fun, satisfying, and worthwhile. They are priced so that acquiring an entire library of them is affordable. And they are beginning readers with a difference—they're written on five levels.

Early Step into Reading Books are designed for brand-new readers, with large type and only one or two lines of very simple text per page. **Step 1 Books** feature the same easy-to-read type as the Early Step into Reading Books, but with more words per page. **Step 2 Books** are both longer and slightly more difficult, while **Step 3 Books** introduce readers to paragraphs and fully developed plot lines. **Step 4 Books** offer exciting nonfiction for the increasingly independent reader.

The grade levels assigned to the five steps—preschool through kindergarten for the Early Books, preschool through grade 1 for Step 1, grades 1 through 3 for Step 2, grades 2 through 3 for Step 3, and grades 2 through 4 for Step 4—are intended only as guides. Some children move through all five steps very rapidly; others climb the steps over a period of several years. Either way, these books will help your child "step into reading" in style!

For Jamie
—C.S.

The editors would like to thank JIM BREHENY, Curator of
Education for the Wildlife Conservation Society at the Bronx Zoo,
and JEFFREY L. NICHOLS, Curator of Education at the Barnum
Museum, for their assistance in the preparation of this book.

Library of Congress Cataloging-in-Publication Data
Worth, Bonnie. Jumbo : the most famous elephant in the world! / by Bonnie Worth ;
illustrated by Christopher Santoro.
    p. cm. — (Step into reading. Step 3 book.)
ISBN 0-375-81014-5 (trade) — ISBN 0-375-91014-X (lib. bdg.)
1. Jumbo (Elephant)—Juvenile literature. 2. Circus—Juvenile literature.
[1. Jumbo (Elephant). 2. Elephants. 3. Circus.]
I. Santoro, Christopher, ill. II. Title. III. Series. GV1831.E4 W67 2001
791.3'2'0929—dc21   00-032799

www.randomhouse.com/kids

Printed in the United States of America   April 2001   10 9 8 7 6 5 4 3 2 1

Step into Reading®

JUMBO
THE MOST FAMOUS ELEPHANT IN THE WORLD!

by Bonnie Worth
illustrated by Christopher Santoro

A Step 3 Book

Random House 🏠 New York

Chapter One

Up and down the streets of a small American town, voices cry out, "They're here!"

All summer long, people have been waiting for this day. They have read the handbills and the stories in the newspapers. They have seen the posters pasted up on fences and barns. In every diner and shop around town, it is all anybody can talk about. And now the day is finally here. The circus has come to town!

But this is not just *any* circus. It is Barnum & Bailey's Greatest Show on Earth! It is the biggest and best circus in the whole world. It has traveled here by train from New York City, where crowds swarmed to see it. Now it is touring the country, stopping in a different town almost every day.

The circus travels by night and arrives in the morning. Its workers set up all day and perform in the evening. The next day, they're off to another town.

Men, women, and children run to the tracks to watch the circus train unload. It is the longest train most of them have ever

seen, with over one hundred railroad cars. Some are brightly painted. Others are plain. *What do they carry?*

The cars carry tent poles and canvas and ropes and banners and bleachers for the crowds to sit in. The cars carry costumes and musical instruments and circus wagons and trapezes and even a cannon! The cars carry clowns and acrobats and singers and dancers and horseback riders and animal trainers. The cars carry horses and zebras and camels and ostriches and snakes and thirty elephants. And then there is the most special car of all.

The special car is extra big and extra sturdy. It is forty feet long, eighteen and a half feet high, and has huge double doors. It is painted gold and red and across it in fancy letters is written JUMBO PALACE CAR. Everybody in town knows who is inside.

They know from the handbills and the

newspaper stories and the posters. They know because Phineas T. Barnum, the co-owner of the circus, made sure they'd know. Inside the car is Barnum's "Towering Monarch Mastodon—the largest and noblest animal on the face of the earth." Inside is Jumbo the Elephant.

Later that evening, crowds line the streets to watch the circus parade by torchlight.

All the performers and animals march through town to a vacant lot, where they put up a giant tent called the Big Top. The circus band leads the way, followed by horses in feathered headdresses. Then come the sideshow acts: Jo-Jo the Dog-Faced Boy, the Chinese Giant, and the Bearded Lady. Next come the clowns, the

jugglers, the snake charmer, the tattooed man, the human cannonball, Zarah the Tightrope Walker, and an entire tribe of Zulus! Then come the thirty elephants, plodding and swaying. And finally, the star of the show.

The crowd gasps, then falls silent.

The posters show him standing thirty feet tall. In reality, he is only eleven and a half feet. Still, the crowd is not disappointed. Jumbo looks *enormous*— bigger than all the other elephants that came before. He is bigger than any living thing anybody there has ever seen. With his long snaking trunk and his huge flapping ears and his four legs like great gray tree trunks, he is an awesome sight.

The children are amazed. Thrilled. They are looking at a living wonder. When they grow up, they will tell their children and their children's children that they once saw the mighty Jumbo.

How did this magnificent African elephant come to be walking down the street of a small town in America? It is a long, sometimes sad, but fascinating story.

Chapter Two

Around 1860, in the wilds of central
Africa, a baby elephant was born. The
little elephant probably lost his mother at
an early age. Little elephants all over
Africa were losing their mothers, and their
fathers, too. *Why?* Because these were the
days before there were laws against the
hunting and killing of elephants. These
were the days when hunters killed
elephants by the hundreds.

Elephants, if left alone, are peaceful
creatures. *So why did people kill them?*
Sometimes for meat. But mostly for their
tusks. Tusks are the elephant's long upper
teeth, which it uses to peel bark from trees

and dig up roots to eat. Tusks are made of
ivory—a smooth, hard, white substance
that people have always prized. The
ancient Greeks used ivory in their
sculpture. During the Middle Ages, it was
used to make holy objects. In the 1800s, it
was used to make more common things,
like fishhooks and pool cues and piano
keys. A single set of tusks could fetch a
hunter over a thousand dollars.

The little elephant might have grown up and been killed for his tusks, but he had a different fate. Collectors came to Africa to catch animals and sell them to zoos. In those days, zoos were even more popular than they are today. Every big city in Europe had a zoo. Lions and tigers were in great demand. So were rhinoceroses and elephants.

An animal collector caught the little elephant, shipped him up the Nile River, and sold him to the Paris Zoo. At the time, the little elephant was only four feet tall.

The little African elephant was now one of many elephants in the Paris Zoo's collection. No one thought he was very special. They kept him in a small, dark, dirty shed. They didn't feed him very well. They didn't wash him very often. They didn't pay much attention to him at all. He might have wasted away in the Paris Zoo, but the little elephant got lucky.

The London Zoo had plenty of Asian elephants, but no African elephants. In fact, there had never been an African elephant in all of England. The London Zoo wanted to be the first zoo in England with an African elephant.

What is the difference between the two kinds of elephants? Asian elephants are smaller than African elephants. They have smaller ears, and their trunks have only one "finger" at the end. African elephants have two "fingers."

As it happened, the Paris Zoo had plenty of Asian *and* African elephants. What it really wanted was a rhinoceros. So the London Zoo traded one of its rhinoceroses for the little African elephant—and two anteaters!

It was the little elephant's first step toward becoming a star.

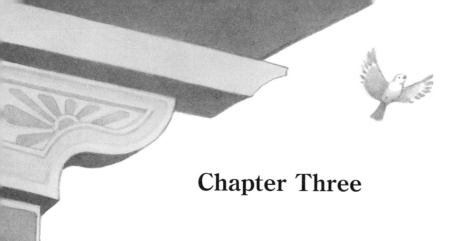

Chapter Three

When Abraham Bartlett—the head of the
London Zoo—opened the crate containing
the new little elephant, he was shocked
and disgusted.

The elephant was filthy and much too
thin. His toenails were long, his hide was
covered with sores, and he was too sick to
eat. Bartlett set to work cleaning the

elephant, trimming his nails, and treating the sores on his hide. Soon the little elephant looked better and felt hungry.

Bartlett fed the little elephant as much as he could eat. He ate hay and straw and rice and beets and bread and green vegetables. The little elephant grew and grew and grew…

…and grew!

In a few short years, the little elephant had grown into a GREAT BIG ELEPHANT —the biggest elephant anyone in England had ever seen.

Bartlett named the elephant Jumbo, after the expression "mumbo jumbo," which meant African magic. It seemed like a good name for the enchanting elephant from Africa.

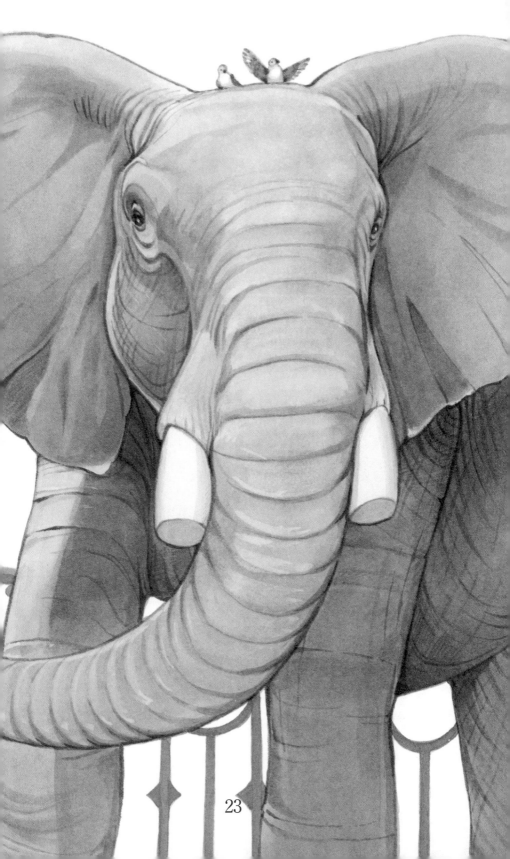

Jumbo became the star of the London Zoo. Every day, he plodded along the garden paths, carrying children on a wooden bench on his back.

During the next fifteen years, over a million children waited in line to ride Jumbo at the London Zoo. Some were famous. Young Teddy Roosevelt had his picture taken on Jumbo's back. So did young Winston Churchill. But whether they were famous or not, rich or poor, Jumbo liked all the children. He never hurt a single one. But the person he liked most in all the world was a man named Matthew Scott.

Matthew Scott worked at the zoo. He was Jumbo's keeper and best friend. Jumbo trusted Scott and Scott trusted Jumbo. Scott fed Jumbo and washed him and even slept with him! Every night before they went to bed, they shared a bottle of beer.

One night, Scott forgot to share his beer and went to sleep. Jumbo lifted Scott with his trunk and shook him! Scott woke up ten feet off the ground! He never forgot to share again.

Jumbo spent his days in peace and contentment. But when he was about twenty years old, something happened that would change his life forever.

Chapter Four

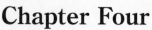

Gentle Jumbo began to get very, very
grumpy. He behaved well in the garden
with the children. But in his house, he
sometimes flew into rages. He bellowed
and he bashed his tusks against the wall
until they cracked and broke. He rubbed
against the bars until his hide was raw.
Sometimes he was even mean to Scott.
What was wrong with Jumbo?

Actually, nothing was wrong. What was happening to Jumbo was natural. The fact is, Jumbo had grown into a mature elephant. Mature male elephants have a gland on each side of their heads. For a few weeks every year, the glands ooze a dark, oily substance, signaling that the elephant is ready to mate. This time is called musth (pronounced *must*).

Today, people know that an elephant in musth should not be bothered. But in those days, they just assumed Jumbo had become dangerous. And that frightened them.

If Jumbo could behave this badly in his house, maybe one day he would behave this badly in the garden—with children on his back! Abraham Bartlett was very worried.

So Bartlett could not have been happier when a man offered him a whopping $10,000 for the agitated elephant. That man was Phineas T. Barnum. Bartlett's six-and-a-half-ton problem now belonged to him.

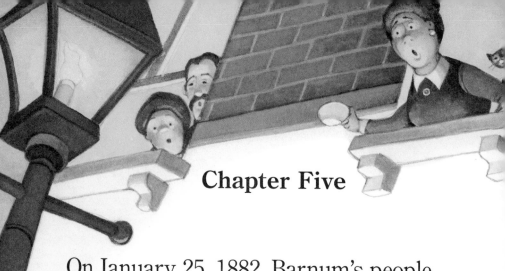

Chapter Five

On January 25, 1882, Barnum's people came with a huge packing crate to load up Jumbo and ship him to America. Crowds of Londoners gathered to watch. But Jumbo would not get into the crate. They tried to coax him, but Jumbo would not budge. Day after day, the crowds gathered to watch, and day after day, Jumbo was having none of it.

The news hit the papers. If Jumbo wouldn't enter the crate, the story went, that meant he didn't want to leave London! Angry letters began to pour into the zoo. *Don't make Jumbo leave!* wrote thousands of British children. *We'll miss you, Jumbo!*

Let the American showman keep his money! Let London keep Jumbo!

In America, Barnum heard about the letters. *Was he upset about the fuss?* Absolutely not! Barnum couldn't have been happier. He was a showman who loved nothing better than a big fuss. Big fusses meant big publicity. And big publicity sold tickets. Americans were more eager than ever to see the latest addition to Barnum's show.

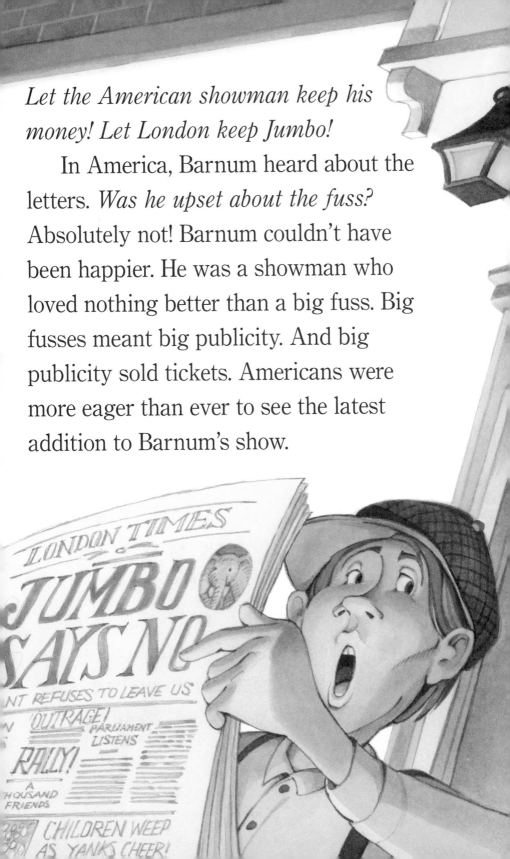

LONDON TIMES

JUMBO SAYS NO

NT REFUSES TO LEAVE US

'OUTRAGE! PARLIAMENT LISTENS

RALLY!

A THOUSAND FRIENDS

CHILDREN WEEP AS YANKS CHEER!

Finally, in March, the problem was solved. It was agreed that Jumbo's keeper, Scott, would come with the elephant to America. With Scott leading the way, Jumbo finally climbed into the crate. It took six horses twenty-four hours to drag him to the dock. There Jumbo was hoisted by crane into the hold of a ship that would sail him to America.

The great elephant and Scott were leaving behind an amazing thing. That thing was Jumbomania.

England had, over the last few months, gone crazy for Jumbo. He was all people talked about. There were discussions in Parliament about whether the zoo had the right to sell him. Even Queen Victoria mourned the loss of this national treasure. There were songs written about Jumbo, and restaurants served Jumbo puddings

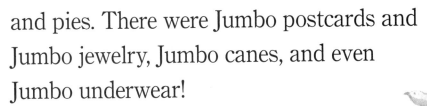

and pies. There were Jumbo postcards and Jumbo jewelry, Jumbo canes, and even Jumbo underwear!

By the time the two travelers had crossed the Atlantic, Jumbomania was there to greet them in New York.

Chapter Six

On April 9, 1882, Barnum & Bailey's Greatest Show on Earth opened at Madison Square Garden, with Jumbo as the star.

What was Jumbo's act? Did he do tricks? No. The horses and lions and tigers did tricks. *Did he work?* No. The camels and the other elephants worked, carrying and pushing and pulling heavy loads. Jumbo was simply a star. He wore a cape and plumed headdress and paraded around the three rings of the circus, impressing people with his enormous size. The crowds loved him.

It had cost Barnum $30,000 to buy

Jumbo and ship him to America. Jumbo
made the money back in his first ten days
in America. He drew the greatest crowds
in circus history.

Every day, Jumbo ate:
    200 pounds of hay
    3 quarts of onions
    2 bushels of rolls
    2 bushels of oats
    3 loaves of bread
    2 crates of fruit and
        cakes and candies
    5 buckets of water
He was treated like a king!

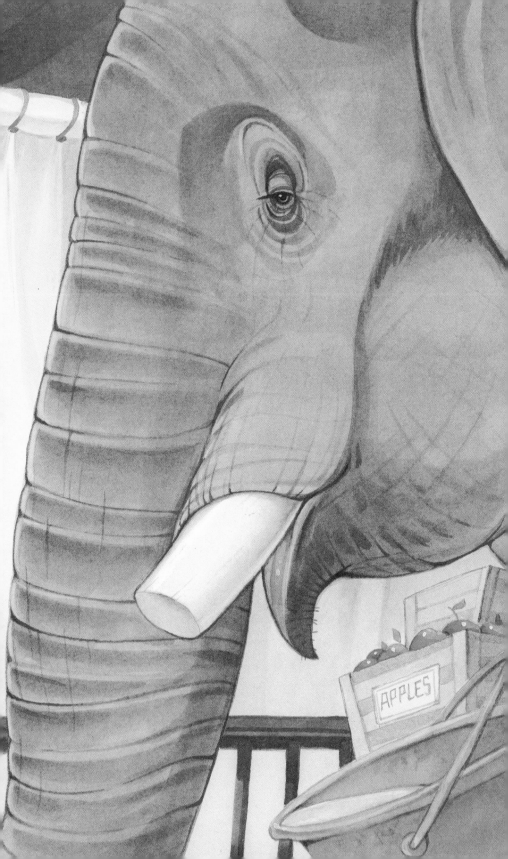

Chapter Seven

Every summer, Barnum & Bailey loaded their circus onto railroad cars and toured it around North America.

It was toward the end of the 1885 season that the circus came to a small town in Canada.

Jumbo had just given the last performance of the day and he—along with all the other elephants—was walking from the tent back to the train. Scott was leading the group with Jumbo and a little elephant called Tom Thumb. Suddenly, as if from out of nowhere, came the headlight of an oncoming train. It blew a loud warning whistle.

Scott tried to steer Jumbo and Tom away from the train, but the light and noise made them panic. Jumbo lifted his trunk and let out a loud trumpet. It was the last sound he would ever make.

The train first crashed into Tom
Thumb. The little elephant was scooped
up by the cowcatcher and flung down a
steep bank. He broke his leg. Then the
train crashed into Jumbo. The train hit him
so hard that it ran off the rails. Holding
the weeping Scott's hand in his trunk,
Jumbo died minutes later.

People around the world mourned the loss of the great elephant. *Did P. T. Barnum mourn?* In his own way, perhaps. He certainly mourned the loss of Jumbo's income. Barnum quickly arranged to have Jumbo stuffed. In fact, it was not long before he was touring with *two* Jumbos— the stuffed hide and the mounted skeleton. The great elephant turned out to be worth more dead than he had been alive.

Chapter Eight

Jumbo is gone, but his name lives on in the dictionary as a word meaning something very large.

Toward the end of his life, Barnum donated Jumbo's stuffed hide to Tufts University in Massachusetts. It was destroyed in a fire in 1975. Athletes at Tufts reportedly rub a peanut butter jar holding Jumbo's ashes for good luck. Jumbo's skeleton is at the American Museum of Natural History in New York City, but sadly it is no longer on display.

The story of Jumbo, sad as it is, touches on issues even larger than the great elephant himself. In the 1970s, there were about 1.3 million elephants in Africa. Twenty years later, there were less than half that many, because hunters were still killing them for their tusks. Fortunately, steps were taken to protect the elephants. Land was set aside for parks and reserves, where they could live freely, and their numbers began to grow again.

Today, elephants are on the endangered species list. There are international laws that protect elephants and control the trade of ivory. There are also laws that prevent elephants in zoos and circuses from being mistreated or placed in unnecessary danger. In ancient times, the elephant was held sacred—and even today, it still is in some places. In the future, it is important that we continue to respect and preserve elephants. We must do all that is within our power to protect, for generations to come, "the largest and noblest animal on the face of the earth."

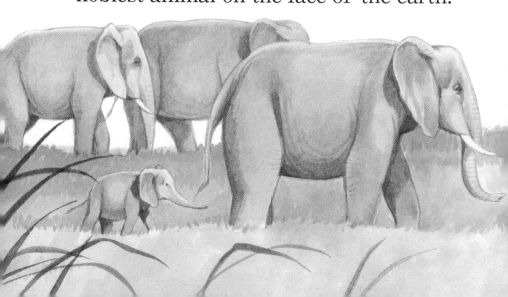